POLICE

CONFIDENTIAL

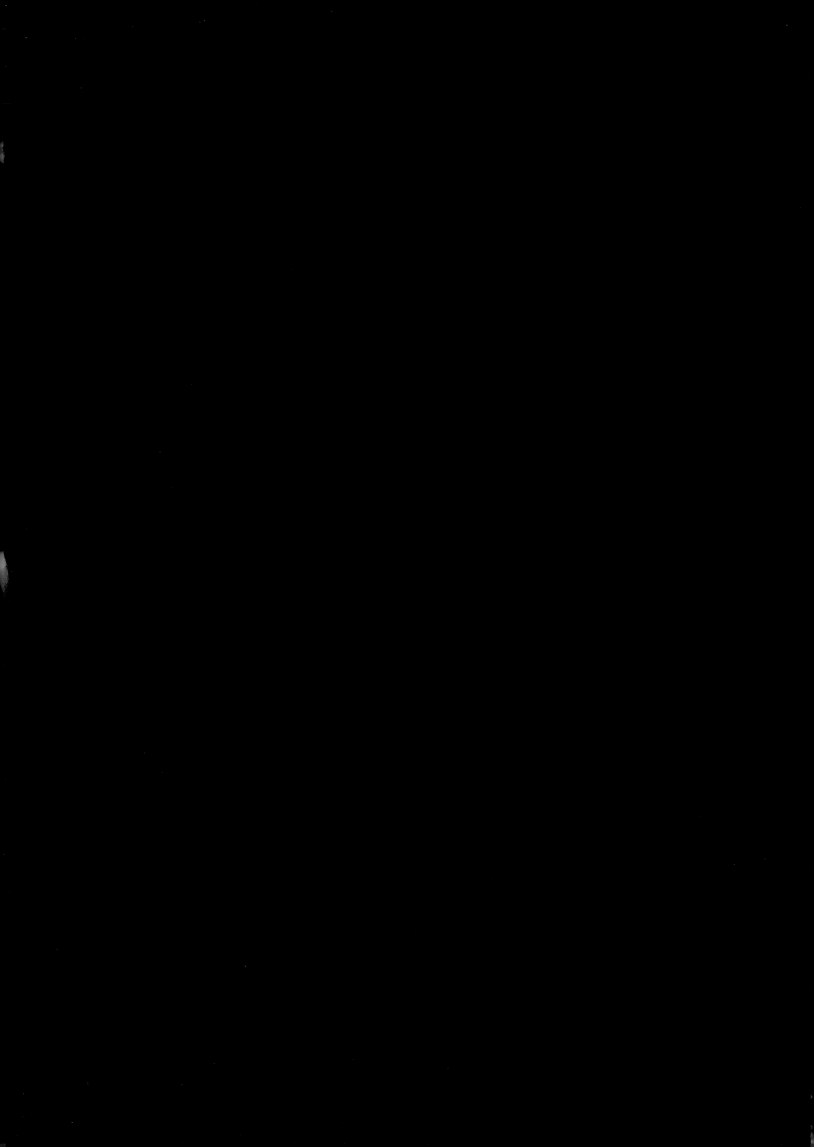

POLICE
CONFIDENTIAL

PHOTOGRAPHS BY DANNY QUATROCHI
INTRODUCTION BY STING
CAPTIONS BY THE POLICE

BTB
BEECH TREE BOOKS
A QUILL EDITION
New York

LIBRARY OF CONGRESS CATALOG CARD NUMBER: 85-72652
ISBN: 0-688-06527-9
0-688-06144-3 (PBK).

EDITED AND COMPILED BY:

JODI PECKMAN

DESIGN:

MANHATTAN DESIGN/OLINSKY & GORMAN
PRODUCTION: CHERI DORR

PHOTO PRINTING:

PAMELA LANDAU

THANK YOU:

MILES COPELAND AND KIM TURNER

PRINTED IN THE UNITED STATES OF AMERICA
FIRST BEECH TREE BOOKS/QUILL EDITION

1 2 3 4 5 6 7 8 9 10

BTB

The word "book" is said to derive from *boka*, or beech.
The beech tree has been the patron tree of writers since ancient times and
represents the flowering of literature and knowledge.

For my Dad

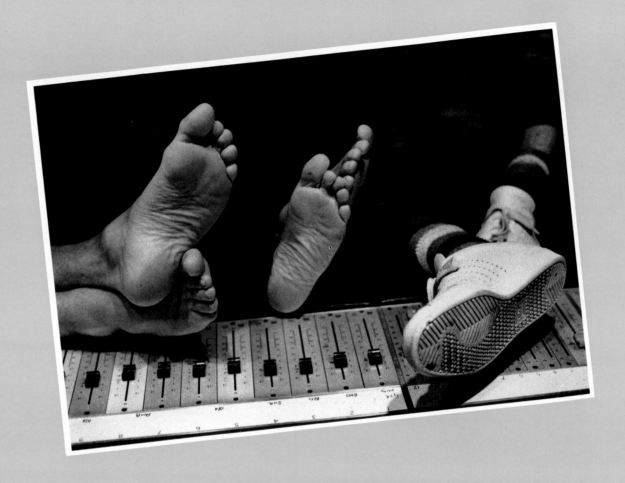

To Sting, Andy and Stewart,
who have given me much more than
the visual source for this book.

As I write this, I'm on a 747 bound for London at about 30,000 feet above the Atlantic. Danny is seated right next to me as usual. We've travelled around this globe together more times than I care to remember. He's asleep at the moment. He's really good value. He sleeps so deeply that you can put all kinds of stuff on him without him waking up. I've taped cutlery to his forehead, dressed him up in funny hats, given him ridiculous false noses. Once I taped a light bulb in his fist.

Really, the best pictures that ever came out of Danny's camera were taken by me, when Danny was asleep in some public place and I dressed him up in something ridiculous. The guy is such a deep sleeper that he wouldn't find out what I'd done to him until he'd got the contact sheets back from the printer.

Now some of you might think this is cruel. However, I must point out that I too have been the victim of this ritual. I remember waking up one morning taped to an air hostess. The pictures will of course appear in my own photo book, along with the humiliating pictures of Danny and compromising shots of Andy and Stewart. Danny also wants me to attempt a biography of him, so let's see...

Danny Quatrochi was born in Jersey City, N.J., on June 25, 1954. He went to school at Roxbury High School in Succasunna, N.J. His father had been a classmate of Frank Sinatra.

Danny worked as a cashier in a foodstore. He ran a machine in a plastic-mold factory. He managed a 7/11 store. At night he played in bands around New Jersey. He quit playing guitar and took up engineering sound for Jersey bands.

In October '79, he got a phone call to work for an unknown English band called The Police. He was interviewed at the Iroquois Hotel on 44th St., by one Kim Turner, who claimed to be the road manager of The Police.

Mr. Turner offered him the job on the spot, providing he could start right away and carry three boxes of tee shirts and a Marshall 4 by 12 cabinet down 11 flights of stairs to the street below, as the lift was broken. By the 9th floor, Quatrochi was having second thoughts.

When he eventually got everything onto the sidewalk, Turner pressed a prepaid air ticket into his hand and told him to get the stuff to Miami by that night. He gave him the address of a gig and then vanished in a cloud of dust.

Second thoughts had been compounded into grave doubts when successive taxi drivers refused to pick him up. Finally someone who was new to the job took pity on the youth and ferried him to Kennedy Airport.

He was forced to convince an airline employee that the loudspeaker and the boxes of tee shirts were his legitimate baggage. A lesser soul would have given up and gone home to Jersey. But a voice somewhere inside his head told him that by perservering with this journey against all the logical reasons why he shouldn't, he would be rewarded in some way. There was the promise of change, of unknown horizons, of some vague, inexplicable glory.

He'd been lugging the boxes of tee shirts and the impossibly heavy speaker cabinet the length of America's eastern seaboard. He'd argued with and eventually bribed a taxi driver to take him and his precious cargo to some dubious juke joint where the band was playing. He hustled his way past the bouncers at the stage door and through a packed club with his three loads, backward and forward through curses, threats and insults and was now knocking on the dressing room door. Bloodied, exhausted but victorious, he manufactured a smile from deep inside somewhere. The door opened.

"Hi, I'm Danny. Kim sent me from New York with this stuff." The door was slammed in his face.

"Get a haircut!"

The band was comprised of a lanky American drummer named Stewart Copeland, a diminutive guitarist named Andy Summers and something in the middle that called itself Sting.

It was Sting who eventually cut Quatrochi's hair, his luscious shoulder length locks were reduced to a brutal 1/4-inch-reform school cut that Sting described as elegant. To Danny it felt like murder. He purchased his first large hat. However...

It was only after this that Danny was accepted into the fold, although he did resist the plan to have him lowered head first into a bucket of peroxide.

The Police then went on to conquer the world, or at least that's what they told everybody. Danny went from drum roadie to guitar tuner to technician, nursemaid to confidante.

In 1980 the band visited Japan (the land of technology and gifts) where someone gave the boys cameras. Andy of course went on to become a brilliant photographer. Sting became bored with the toy after half an hour. Focusing was such a drag (his career as a brilliant photographer wasn't to begin until the advent of the automatic focus), and he also realized that if you were taking pictures, you couldn't be in them. So he gave the camera to Danny so that he could become a brilliant photographer. Stewart Copeland left his camera on a train.

After this the band toured places that no band had ever been before, for no apparent reason, and Danny of course was there snapping away. Occasionally Sting would want his camera back, saying that he needed to take some pictures of his feet. But the focusing got the better of him and Danny would get the camera back after five minutes.

However, to return to the main issue. When Danny isn't sleeping, or helping me schlep around the airports of the world, he's usually behind a camera preserving moments that would be lost forever to my memory. But every picture tells a story, and entraps a moment of madness, joy, exhaustion or sadness that only a trusted friend would be able to capture.

I hope you enjoy this book as much as I have.

I'm going to wake Danny up now and present him with this introduction. It'll help him get over the swizzle sticks I taped to his ears.

Love,

ZENYATTA

MONDATTA

A Police moment - in three stages

Javelin practice, it took
us half an hour to pull
it out of the wall

If you make a mistake, play it again, but keep a straight face

'80–'81   ZENYATTA TOUR   IN FRANCE WITH BILL WYMAN

A contented moment with
the second best thing
in life: Food.

Japan - 1st time round.
I remember the coat.

SUMMER–FALL '81   STING IN HOLLAND, FRANCE, SPAIN

ASLEEP IN PERTH AIRPORT

FALL '81   STEWART BACKSTAGE

Andy in a coat (made by his mom)

FEBRUARY '80   SYDNEY, AUSTRALIA   SOUND CHECK OUTSIDE SHOW

34

36

An interview with
the DRIBBLE TWINS

Another Winter of Discontent

GHOST IN

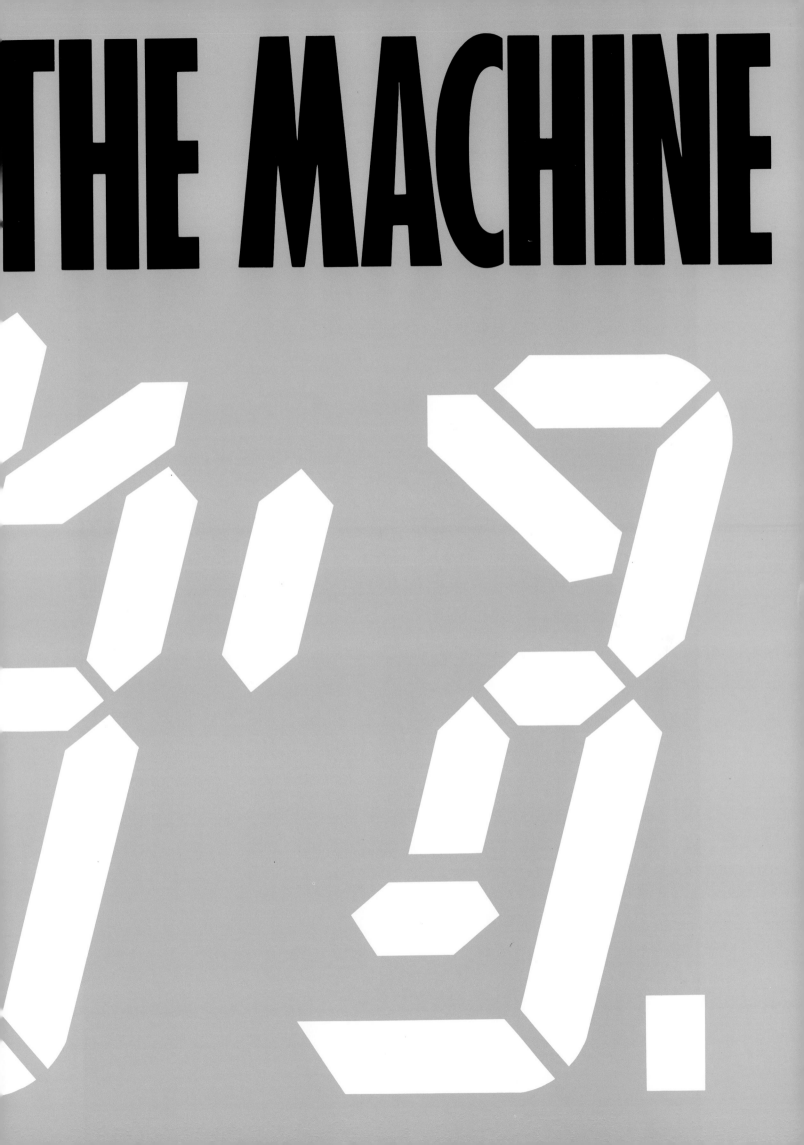

Crab racing in Montserrat

44

This 'BAREDA'S Just isn't what it useo to be

AH ' thats better

JUNE '81   AT THE BEACH IN MONTSERRAT

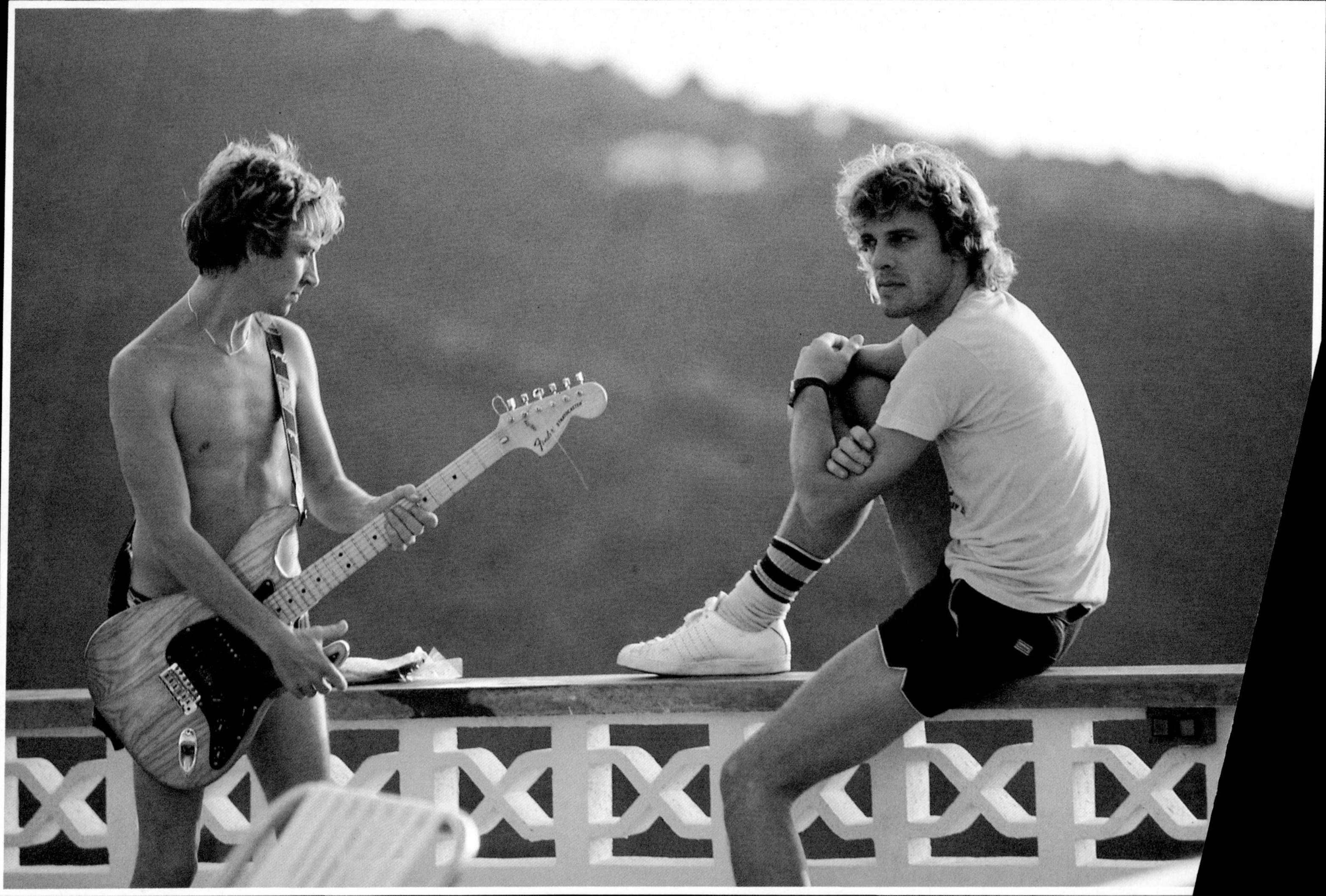
Fender
STRATOCASTER

MILES COPELAND, THE BAND'S MANAGER

STING AT GHOST SESSIONS

52

this was taken aboard a 1943 Dakota.
One hour later we were almost "wiped
out", it started to fall to pieces in
a hurricane.

MAY '81   ANDY AT AIR STUDIOS

Is the green light on yet?

Pregig tension

the charts in the background
are notes for further work
on the tracks: Cymbal
overdub ; Thicken chorus;
try Andy singing it; that
sort of thing. Andy's head
is obscured

61

Tea - Vicar

64

Doing charitable work in an old peoples home.

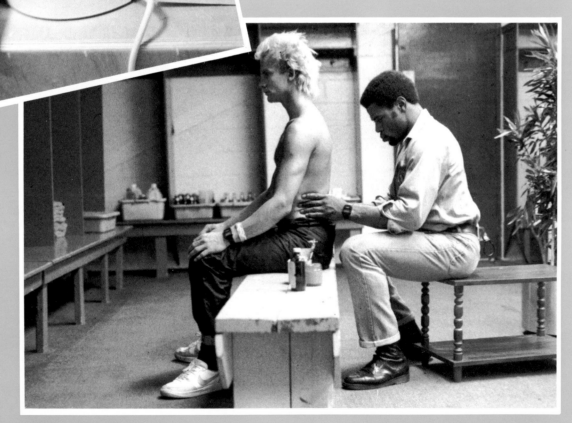

STING USED THIS DEVICE TO CLEAR AND LOOSEN HIS LUNGS AND THROAT BEFORE A SHOW.

Yeah mum, everythings going real well, bye!

John would lift me above his head and then put me down really gently.

68

Self provocation in an idle moment with Japanese subtitles. Jeff Seitz is adjusting my earings

STING ONSTAGE, TOOTING BEC, FALL '81   STEWART AT GHOST SESSIONS, SUMMER '81

F#, B no Ab. who cares, no-one's here anyway!

STEWART, SOUND CHECK, FALL '81

Uh-oh, the chin is out
and I'm looking down stage
right.

73

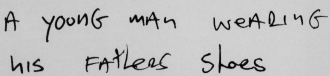

A YOUNG MAN WEARING
his FATHERS shoes

SUMMER '81   MONTSERRAT   GHOST SESSIONS

SYNCHRONICITY

STING AT REHEARSALS IN LOS ANGELES, SPRING '83   STEWART PLAYING POLO

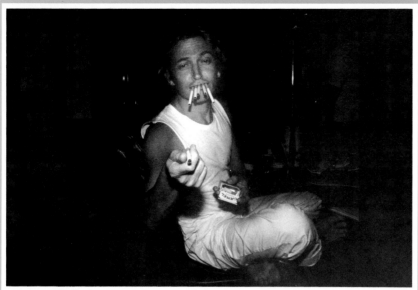

A SnAP of the SURGEON GERRAL
— In A RELAXED moment

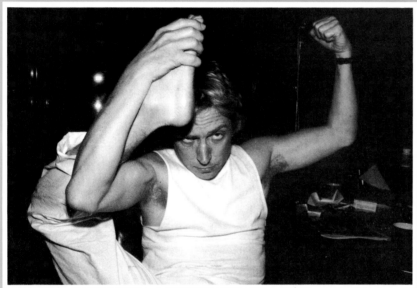

EAt your heart out JAne Fonda!

I ~~must stop~~ EATING At ~~McDONALDS~~
OR I LEARNED this FROM a girc in PittsBURG
OR POSITION 3,672 FROM the KAMASUTRA

happy birthday to me

Which end do you look through?

BALLS!

86

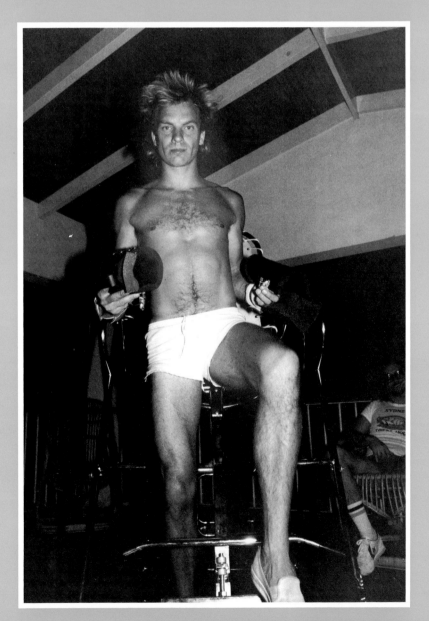

ON THE GRAVITY GUIDANCE MACHINE

Ready when you are Mr De Mille!

I DISTINCTLY ORDERED BIRDS NEST SOUP

Ol' BLUE eyes is BACK

NOBLE, with A DEFINITE SENSE
OF street CRED

Testing the first pair of flying underpants

DUNE

99

Here's a shot of me shrinking
Brad Dourif.

They dyed my hair orange
for Dune, people said I
looked like Woody Wooopecker.

103

Thinks! I wonder if his make up is contagious?

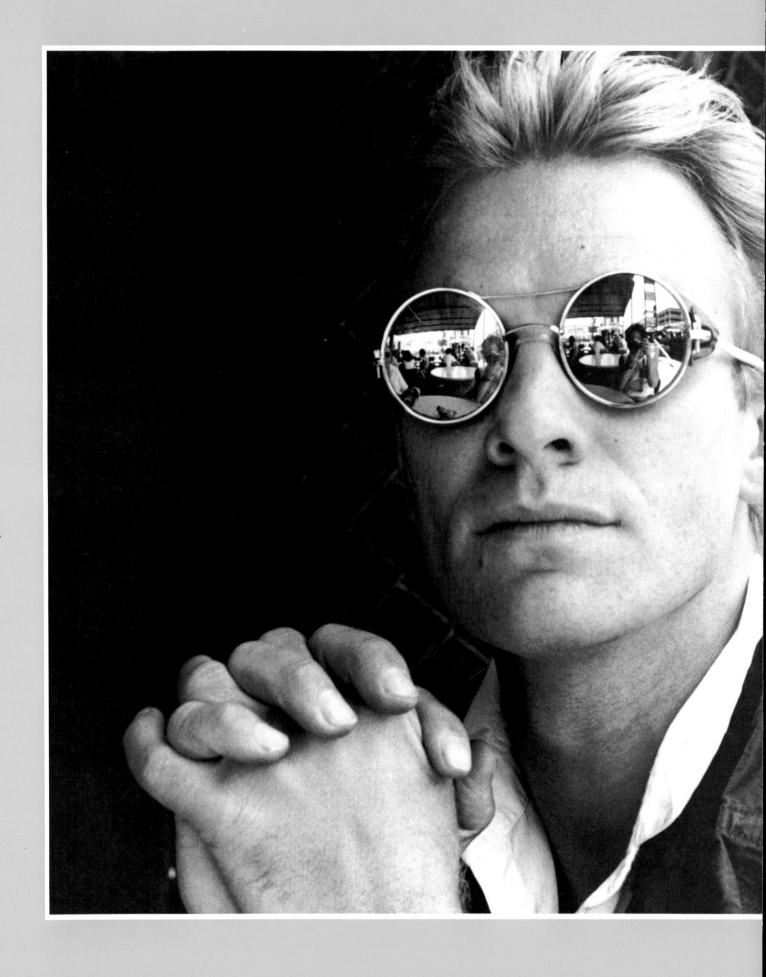

JUNE '83   MEXICO CITY

JUNE '83   MEXICO CITY   FLEA MARKET   HOTEL ROOM

A popular restaurant
in Mexico

The guy at the back is her husband,
he later tried to strangle me

How the hell did I get myself into this mess?

this is me at the top of the largest meat
the inca's used to throw sacraficial victims

renderizer in the world.

rom the top and then eat them.

SYNCHRONICITY

Band motto "Less is More"

not tonight love —

"I've got a headache"

this is when I used to be called Nike

I wean Sting in a lovely
Andy ~~Andy~~ 1940ʳˢ FASHION SHOT!

A LiHLe OFF the Shoulder number

Julian is wearing a lovely
SPRING FASHION of foot PLASTERS
goggles + what's that on his head

A stunning moment
of Rock Power

Down A Bit ?

Hows this ?

I speak fluent dog.
this was taken
...wing a
...onversation with
Willie.

One of DURAN DURAN DURAN

SO? WLERE ARE THE BAGELS?

118

STEWART AT AIR STUDIOS   STING AT REHEARSAL IN LOS ANGELES   ANDY ON SYNCHRONICITY TOUR

Rehearsing for Sync tour
at the Worried Rabbit.
After a long lay off we
sounded like a high school
band. A week later we
sounded like a college
group. It took about three
weeks to sound world famous.

STING AND WILLIE DOING DEMOS AT A
RECORDING STUDIO IN NEWCASTLE

This is me giving my horse Sandaly
Some last minute advice before winning
a race at Newbury Racecourse

Dear Mum, 'do you
think you could come
over and darn a
pair of my socks.

Hampstead Fair 84:
   Its the only way I can get
my hair to stick up.

After this shot was taken those girls behind me started makin a fuss of Willie, my dog. What they were really doing was finding out my adress from his ident. tag.
I had to move house

STING AND TRUDIE,
BACKYARD, STING'S HOME
IN LONDON.

SUMMER '84   HAMPSTEAD HEATH, LONDON

Stig and Andy cash got percusions racks like these to decorate their living rooms

After all these years I still can't keep my eyes open and play, I feel more cheerfull then I look.

125

Mauri welcome Auckland
New Zealand

Nureyev - accompanied by Sting & Stewart